AF379654

Spiritual
Chocolate

Spiritual Chocolate

for the
Christmas Season

Dr. Glenn Mollette

GMA & Inspiration Press
Newburgh, Indiana

Acknowledgements

For Karen who was always incredible at making the house festive during the Christmas season.

For Mom and Dad who were always good to me at Christmas.

For Jared and Zachary who have always been God's gift to me at Christmas.

For the many friends and family members that I have celebrated Christ's birth with over the years.

Contents

CHAPTER ONE

The Life of Christmas

Luke 2: 4 7, "So Joseph also went up from the town of Nazareth in Galilee to Judea, to Bethlehem the town of David, because he belonged to the house and line of David. He went there to register with Mary, who was pledged to be married to him and was expecting a child. While they were there the time came for the baby to be born, and she gave birth to her firstborn, a son, she wrapped him in cloths and placed him in a manger, because there was no room for them in the inn."

Christmas brings feelings.

Mary felt overwhelming amazed – spellbound by the announcement of her pregnancy. The shepherds were - surprised.

How do you feel about Christmas?

Excited? – I use to get really excited about the Christmas season. Santa Claus is coming - right?

Dread? Here it comes again.

Amazed? Is Christmas not amazing?

Anticipation? Family, friends.

Disappointed… 'The gifts are unwrapped. Well Christmas is over." It is?

Depression… I'll be home for Christmas if only in my dreams. I'll have a Blue Christmas without you.

What about loneliness on Christmas? Will you be alone on Christmas? Think about others who may be alone on Christmas. Why don't you invite them over? Spend part of the day together. You might be pleasantly surprised how many might respond.

Joseph was disappointed. How could this have happened to me? Why did this happen to me? During this season of the year we are prone to be more reflective. We are likely to look more introspectively.

Christmas was kind of like this the first year. Herod was mad about Christmas. Someone else was being sought out for worship. Someone else was about to receive accolades. And Herod couldn't stand it.   Can you share Christmas? Or is Christmas all about you? Is it all about what you get? Is it all about what you have under the tree? Is Christmas all about the size or the price? Who are the gold, frankincense and myrrh for? Well…Herod…don't take it personally…but it's for someone else. We don't see any place in the Bible where the Wise Men had any animosity toward Herod. They had come to Bethlehem for a higher purpose.

But Simeon was a righteous man, devout who had waited all his life for the coming of Christ. Luke 2:25 "He was waiting for the consolation of Israel, and the Holy Spirit was upon him. It had been revealed to him by the Holy Spirit that he would not die before he had seen the Lord's Christ. Moved by the Spirit, he went into the temple courts. When the parents brought in the child Jesus to do for him what the custom of the law required, Simeon took him in his arms and praised God, saying: "Sovereign Lord, as you have promised, you now dismiss your servant in peace. For my eyes have seen your salvation, which you have prepared in the sight of all people."

This Christmas, do not overlook the purpose. Consider, *The Life of Christmas* – is the reality of Christmas. Christmas is real. Christmas is real because Jesus is real.

When Mary gave birth …she gave birth to reality. The gospel of John says in chapter one, "The word became flesh and dwelt among us." Prophecy became life. Word became reality. Expectancy came into existence. What had been predicted and prophesied now had come to pass. When Jesus was in the manger…there was life in the manger. Before …all there had been were a few smelly animals and straw and manure. Life was more than ordinary. Now …the ordinary became the extraordinary. God had been born. God was in the cow's trough. And that ordinary stable became transformed into the most special spot in all of creation. No longer was the stable ordinary. The stable now was extraordinary. And it was all because God had entered this mundane place in a very incredible way - birth through a common woman who could be used by God.

The life of Christmas is not the stable. But what came to dwell in the stable. The life of Christmas is not an old rough cow's trough. But what was laid in the trough. The life of

Christmas was not peasant parents. But parents that God could use.

Today let us be reminded that the life of Christmas is not a house. But it's who is in the house. It's not a tree, decorations and surroundings but who is the center of our surroundings. When Jesus was born and placed in that manger He was the center of attention. Mary and Joseph loved him. Shepherds came to see him, Wise men came to adore him, Herod and others were stirred about him. There was no ignoring Jesus. And this Christmas you will not ignore him either. You will worship, adore and love him and experience life or turn your face from him and experience a dull, depressing Christmas.

Jesus is the life of your Christmas. He brought life to Bethlehem. He brought life to bored shepherds. He brought life to wise men who came to worship and he will bring life to you. Simeon was an old prophet who had waited his entire life for the coming of the Lord. When Mary and Joseph took him to the temple, Simeon celebrated the birth of Jesus. Now he could die.

Whether you are almost dead physically – Christ will be your life this Christmas. If you are emotionally drained – Christ will be your life this Christmas. If you are disappointed in yourself, life, depressed…Christ is your life this season.

Do you dread Christmas? Is Christmas a drag to you? We forget what Christmas is about. We dread it because we start thinking – Christmas is a trip to the mall. It's work. It's decorations. It's stress. No. Christmas is a celebration of someone's birthday. Christmas is the day we commonly set aside as Jesus' birthday. Have a little birthday celebration for Jesus.

We are celebrating the day God came to begin the process of purchasing our redemption. It was the beginning of the process. That process would be one of Jesus living. He would live and then he would die and then live again so that we might live with real life. Jesus came to give real life to our world. Jesus is the life of your Christmas.

Jesus is your tomorrow – Suicides happen during the Christmas season. I've often wondered if people could make it one more day. Christ is our one more day. Joseph kept going not because of how he felt but because of the promise of tomorrow. It had been revealed to him that Jesus was truly special. Tomorrow comes for the believer in Christ. It may not be in this life. Our appointment with death may happen today. The body may fail us today. But, Jesus will not fail us. He gives to us eternal life and no man can pluck us from the Father's hand. He gives to us eternal life.

My father slowly walked away from my mother's casket saying, "I don't know how I will go on. But he has. He has a church and a community of friends and loved ones. And he is active. From November 12 through the end of January he killed 90 rabbits. I said, "Dad don't kill them all!" He said, "I am really lonely but God gives me things to do and look forward to." I think my father finds things to look forward to. Now he is 80 years old and has a Honda 4-wheeler. He rides it in the mountains.. So he has something to do and loves his choir at church and he goes there to sing and so there is something to do.

Friend there is something for you to do. God has a tomorrow for you.

The disciples were moping and dragging around. Jesus appeared to Peter and said Peter, "It is time to get over your depression. You failed me. You messed up. You sinned big time. But Peter it's for you and your sins that I came. Get on with life and feed my sheep. At the cross it seemed as though Peter had no life. At the courtyard he wept bitterly. It seemed he could not go on. He could have gone the route of Judas and committed suicide. Judas could not see a tomorrow. But Jesus appeared and commissioned the disciples to go and spread the good news. He wanted them to tell everybody. Peter and all of the disciples went forward and never before had they so much to live for. Jesus became their tomorrow!

The story is told that during the days of Christopher Columbus that most people believed the earth was flat. Some ancient mariners once chiseled some words on that great rock the rock of Gibraltar that said, "No more beyond."

But Columbus came along and said the earth is round and there is more and they had to go back out to the rock of Gibraltar and remove the "no" and left only these words, "More beyond."

Jesus Christ has sailed the sea of death and he come back to tell us, "In my father's house are many mansions." There is much more beyond. Friend, whether your life is here or in heaven. There is more beyond today. There is a tomorrow for every child of God.

Jesus is your promise – we are promised Christ. Simeon saw the promise. Micah 5:2 "But you, Bethlehem,

Ephrathah, though you are small among the clans of Judah, out of you will come for me one who will be ruler over Israel, whose origins are from of old, from ancient times." The Old Testament gave the promise. Simeon lived for the promise. Wise men sought out the promise. Mary realized the promise. Joseph realized the promise. You see God's promises always come true. Jesus was the fulfillment of the promise!

Really? Then why am I so unhappy? Why is my life the way that it is? Why did someone I love die?

We are not promised long life. We are not even promised happiness. We are not promised health. We are not promised huge success. We are not promised riches. We are not promised that all of our dreams or wishes will come true. But we are promised Christ. We are promised a fulfilled life. We are promised eternal life. We are promised riches in heaven. What do you have when your health is gone? My mother had Christ.

When you can't spend the money you've saved? You have Christ. When the person you love more than any other in the world has died you still have Christ.

And in eternity we will always have Christ. Jesus promised that we would have our needs met. Matthew 6:33 "Seek first his kingdom and his righteousness, and all these things will be given to you as well."

And Christmas is great not because we have the tree…the tinsel and decorations…Christmas is great because we have each other…and because we have Jesus. And heaven will be great for the same reason. We will have Jesus and there will be a great reunion time!

But Jesus is our today. When Jesus was born there was life ...at that moment. And Jesus has come to give us this moment. We waste and trivialize the moments of life. We worry about tomorrow and regret the past and mess up today dwelling about things that we can't change or don't know for sure. All we have is today and Jesus is our life for today.

Don't mess up today. Don't mess up this Christmas. Do the best you can. "I have come to give you life and give it to you abundantly," John 14.

There is life for today. There is strength for today. There is hope for today. Our feelings are today. We regret yesterday and fear tomorrow but our feelings are today. And it's our feelings of hope and life today that we have

At most Christmas plays a toy baby is often placed in the manger scene. One Church decided to use a relatively new baby one Christmas and the baby decided he was unhappy and cried through some of the dramatic scenes. Mary picked the baby up and one child was heard in the audience to say, "That baby is real." Friend, Jesus is real.

CHAPTER TWO

Good Will
and Peace to All!

"And suddenly there was with the angel a multitude of the heavenly host praising God and saying, 'Glory to God in the highest, and on earth peace, good will toward men.," (Luke 2: 14). KJV.

The violent act of terrorism toward our country on September 11th was a direct act of war and hostility toward our country. Thousands of innocent lives were killed and families emotionally impaired forever. Our nation will never be the same. The organizers of this horrific act were very successful in communicating to our country their feelings of ill will toward our country. They revealed their evil and hatred to our nation. Our country will never have any grace or sympathy toward anyone remotely connected with terrorism.

How do you extend or create good will?

Do you remember in Genesis chapter 43 that Jacob was sending his children to Egypt for food? They were perishing in the land of Canaan. There was a severe famine. Before they set out, we read that he said in verse 11, "Put some of the best products of the land in your bags and take them down to the man as a gift – a little balm and a little honey, some spices and myrrh, some pistachio nuts and almonds. Take double the amount of silver with you, for you must return the silver that was put back into the mouth of your sacks. Perhaps it was a mistake. Take your brother also and go back to the man at once. And may God Almighty grant you mercy before the man so that he will let your other brother and Benjamin come back with you.

In verse 15, "So the men took the gifts and double the amount of silver, and Benjamin also. They hurried down to Egypt and presented themselves to Joseph."

We very visibly get the picture. The household of Jacob is starving. And now Joseph trying to get all the family together and working for reconciliation keeps Simeon in Egypt in prison. Jacob wants to save his son…he has already lost Joseph he thinks. Therefore, he wants to be in the good favor and grace of this powerful leader in Egypt. His goal is to extend good will …or peace. Therefore he does all that he is able to do to extend good will to Joseph and Egypt.

Our church for many years has decorated an Angel tree for the Christmas season. The big tree has been placed in our fellowship hall and as many as 100 children's names have been placed on the tree to receive a gift. People in our congregation select one or two names from the tree and purchase a gift for the child by the middle of December. Right before Christmas people in our church who oversee the ministry distributes the gifts. Children who normally might not receive anything for Christmas receive nice gifts purchased by the members of our church. The people who give the gifts speak of the blessing they receive in giving. The ones who take the gifts to the families and see the expressions on the faces of the children say they receive the greatest blessing.

The angels told the shepherds on that first Christmas night, "Peace on earth and good will toward men." Peace on earth is so often the result of good will. God through His good will sent His Son to us. He sent Jesus. Jesus came to bring peace to every life that would make room for Him. When you do an act of good will you are setting the stage for peace.

Good will may be a kind word. Good will may be a good deed. Good will may be doing something to help a person in need. It's hard to lash out at someone who brings gifts of good will.

The angels brought an announcement of good will and peace to all men. Jesus Christ was God's miraculous gift of good will, grace and love. We are the very blessed recipients of his favor! Our peace that we enjoy at this holiday season did not come accidentally. Our peace is here because of a very planned effort on the part of God. Down throughout the centuries of time God was planning on his good will to all people. His good will would break down the barriers of sin and ugliness and establish a relationship between He and mankind. Jesus was not an accidental gift of God. Jesus was the calculated plan of God's good will to bring peace on earth.

How might you today calculate good will? Is there someone that you might willfully, purposefully, extend a favor of grace toward? Not all-good will works out. Jesus has been often rejected and even hated by the very people for whom God intended. Yet, for many who have rejected Him and lived lives of being filled with despair there have been many who received him and come to enjoy why he came. Why did he come? He came for peace.

Here are some ways you might extend good will:

1. *Give someone a good word.* Encouragement is always in season. It doesn't have to be the Christmas season. People need encouragement for all season of life. We need it during the teenage years when we are trying to find our way. We need it during the child rearing years when life is pressured and hectic. We need it during old age when we think we are no longer need or forgotten. We need it when we have tried and failed or when we have messed up. Give someone some good will. Words can bless or words can curse. You can help or hinder someone by your language.

2. *Do a good act.* Those who deliver gifts or give a cup of cold water in the name of the Lord are not unnoticed. The book of James reminds us that our Christianity is to be demonstrated by our works. Faith without works is dead.

3. *Give, as you are able.* Jacob gave as he could give. Jesus Christ came from the heart of God. He was God's gift to mankind. He revealed the heart of God. Peace on earth and Good will to all men.

Be a friend. You can only be a close friend to a few people. If you have too many it will deplete and zap your life. But someone that you can relate to may really need you. God saw how much we needed him. That's why he came to us. He came to save us. Your good friendship may be the very good will that makes all the difference in someone's life.

Good will to all men! "Glory to God in the highest, and on earth peace to men on whom his favor rests."

Hot Chocolate and Snow

Snow hasn't stayed long in Southern Indiana. During my eight plus years of living in the region I have seen very few big snows. One comes and there may be three or four inches of accumulation but in three or four days it's gone. A big snowfall is always a possibility but they seldom come. The small snowstorms are usually just enough to slow life down for a day or two. These days give me an excuse to go into a slower more laid back mode. I sip a cup of coffee or may do something I normally would never do – drink a hot cup of chocolate and watch the snowfall.

I'm not a rocking chair kind of guy. It's not been since I was a child sitting on my grandparent's porch that I've ever taken life in a kicked back kind of way. It seems like the snow and messy roads gives me permission to take an hour or two and do nothing but enjoy God's artistic wonders.

A lot can happen in an hour. The snow, the quiet from few cars moving and the tranquility of a hot cup of chocolate gives God a chance to talk. I think God is always talking to us. He speaks to us. He tries to lead us. He wants to instruct us. He often warns us. When we are quiet it is amazing what we can hear God saying.

Joseph was warned by God in a dream to take the baby Jesus and Mary and flee Bethlehem. They went over into Egypt and lived until God led them back. Of course Joseph had been hearing from other sources before. We know God sent an angel to direct him previously when he was reeling in shock from Mary's pregnancy. He knew the child was not his. God sent word to Joseph to proceed with his wedding plans. The child was supernatural…conceived by the Holy Spirit. Joseph listened to the message and proceeded as he had planned and God used him to care for Jesus in his infancy years. We don't know what happened to Joseph later. We don't see him in Jesus' later life or at the cross. He may have died during Jesus' young adult years. Joseph heard from God in the beginning and when Jesus was in danger Joseph was still hearing from God. The fact that he could hear made it possible for God to direct his life. Because God could direct Joseph meant he could also bless Joseph.

There are elementary truths herein. We must be able to hear God. Hearing God strategically positions us to pick the best roads and paths of life. Choosing the best roads leads to blessings. Jesus was spared because God was able to get a word into Joseph.

Our lives are so hectic today. During the Christmas season, life doesn't get slower. It speeds up. When the Thanksgiving holiday comes it seems like we turn our lives up three notches in speed. We go at such a fast pace that we don't really kick back and enjoy what should be a wonderful season.

Often, it's the snowfall that halts us in our fast-paced tracks and makes us do something that requires a different speed – slow speed. There is little that we are use to doing on slow speed. Sitting down with a hot cup of chocolate and taking time to enjoy the snowfall gives God a chance to get a word to us. We have the opportunity to reflect and think about what is really important in life.

We shouldn't wait for inclement weather to do something that is more relaxed, slower and easier. Truthfully, we need these moments every day. Life was never meant to be non-stop running. God built us to sit also. Life was never made for constant speaking. God gave us ears to listen too.

I don't recommend hot chocolate every day. Probably, you should drink it only occasionally. But I do recommend finding a time every day when you listen to God and pray and allow Him to direct your life. He will speak to you…just like he did Joseph. And as he does you will find continued new blessings and direction and help for your life. Remember, God sees our world and our life from a different level. He can see what we cannot see. He knows what we are yet to discover. Go into neutral every day and spend some time with him.

CHAPTER FOUR

Christmas Break

Students love the Christmas break. It's a time away from the books and classes. For a few days longer hours of sleep and some time to do something different than going to school is most welcome. The work force enjoys whatever down time that the holiday brings. Some places may close work for a few days while some may only recognize the Christmas day as vacation.

Everybody needs breaks. A retired person may not see all the big deal about Christmas holidays. When one is in retirement mode, breaks may signify a change of scenery such as a trip more than actual time off from an activity.

The breaks are obvious in the Christmas story. The wise men left home and took a long break. Jesus was two years old when they found him. We don't know they traveled for two years. But it is safe to assume their travel was more than an overnighter to see Jesus.

The shepherds it seems were not away from their flock very long. They were in a nearby field watching their sheep when they received the angelic announcement of Jesus' birth. They took a little time off to see Jesus.

Mary and Joseph ended up being away for sometime. They first traveled to Bethlehem and then after Jesus is a small child they flee to Egypt for His safety.

We all need breaks.

We need breaks from work. Even God rested on the seventh day. I think sometimes that we think there is some kind of special heavenly reward for people who kill themselves working. Is life nothing more than work? There is gratification from work well done. There is fulfillment in the fruit that labor brings. Life is more than work but you'll never know unless you take a break to find out.

We need breaks from the routine. For the shepherds it was a brief break. Yet, even brief moments of doing something different are very refreshing. The daily grind of doing the same old thing wears us down. What we are doing may be very productive and meaningful – but, so routine that we are worn out. The break helps us to run in a different gear. When the break is over we are able to go back into the gear we were previously in and be okay because we feel rested. The change did us good.

We need breaks from people. I can only imagine how good this time away was for Mary and Joseph. They had been through an ordeal. Mary was pregnant out of marriage. The rumor mill had to be a grueling emotional strain to this young couple just trying to start out in life. It had to be mentally refreshing on them to get out of town for a while.

Sometimes people at work, friends or even family take everything out of us. We get tired of the daily interaction that requires a lot of emotion and mental exhaustion. Some of these people may be very close to us. We may even care for or love them. Often the pain of caring for them can just be exhausting and we need a break to replenish our emotional strength. Our physical well being hinges on what is going on within us emotionally and spiritually. We help our bodies when we care for our internal well being.

There are times when we need a family break. We need time with our loved ones. Some of the greatest times in my life have been when I was on a trip with wife and children.

There are times when we need a personal break. I call it a God break. Jesus took time to be by himself. He needed it. There were those times when he needed to just get away from the crowds...go into a remote spot and spend time with His Father.

My idea of a break is packing a few relaxed clothes, exercise shoes, laptop, Bible and then going someplace where I can put all of them into use ...when I want to.

Most people can't handle being alone or going someplace alone. But, how will we ever be able to hear God's still small voice if we aren't alone? How will we find the clear will of God for our lives if we are not alone long enough to tune into what He is saying to us? How will we sort through our feelings, ambitions and moods if we are constantly entertaining someone or have some one daily in our face?

We need a God break. We need the time when all we can do is look and have God in our face and hear what he is trying to say.

I realize we read that the wise men traveled to see Jesus together and the shepherds had the company of each other when they saw Jesus. Jesus even asked his disciples to watch and pray with him. But there are too many instances in scripture when holy men came out of refuge replenished and strengthened for greater service. Elijah needed time alone to be strengthened by God after a long ordeal with Ahab, Jezebel and the false prophets of Baal. God spoke to Moses through the burning bush when Moses was alone and was able to tune in to what God was saying.

There are the times when we need a break to be with others that we love so that we might rekindle and strengthen our relationships. There are times that we need to just be with God so that we might rekindle and strengthen our relationship.

During the Christmas break take a God break. Take time to see Jesus. Take time to experience God's love and feel his presence. It may only be an hour for you on your knees with your bedroom door closed. It may be an afternoon walk in the park. It may be an entire day or days away. You are God's child. You talk to Him about what kind of break you and He needs. He will tell you.

CHAPTER FIVE

Give Strips of Cloth at Christmas

The baby Jesus was wrapped in strips of cloth and placed in a manger.

Mary, like any good mother made provision for the protection of her child. The little baby had been inside her warm womb. Coming into the world naked is like stepping outside of a warm house on a cold day – it can be shocking. Mary as best as she could with what she had, tried to provide for the comfort and safety of her child. The strips of cloth were her motherly effort to care for Jesus. She and Joseph would bind him snugly and then securing straw in the stable they made as warm a bed for their new baby they could possibly make.

Mary and Joseph were special people. God was not going to trust just anybody with His Son. These were two people who had the capability of caring for a baby. They would parent this child and raise him to where he would be the most influential man in the world – ever. Of course, Jesus was God...that helped. Yet, God was looking for special people to care for his son.

Mary and Joseph protected this baby. Every baby needs the protection of loving parents. Babies are helpless. They need food, clothed and given care. They need warmth. They need protection in times of sickness. They can't care for themselves and make themselves well. They need loving parents to help them get better. Jesus would have this kind of parents. When King Herod threatened his life, Joseph had the sense with God's leadership to flee into Egypt. He and Mary protected Jesus.

Mary and Joseph would raise this child. We believe they were committed to this task. We have no reason to really believe Joseph did not do his best. We don't see him in Jesus' latter life. Did Joseph just abandon his family? Did he do as so many men do today – leave his family helpless? I don't believe so. I think Joseph died before Jesus began his public ministry. We don't know for sure. However, Joseph was committed in the early part of Jesus' life. Joseph followed through with the marriage, the birth, the exodus to Egypt and in Jesus' early life we read about Joseph. We see Joseph as the concerned parent looking for his child that he found astonishing the leaders in the temple.

Mary and Joseph did not raise a dumb child. They saw to his education as a child. Jesus was able to astonish the leaders in the temple because his parents saw to his schooling. It's tough. Most children balk at school, homework and books at one time or another. Some balk all the way through every day of school. Jesus grew in wisdom. He studied and applied himself to life. His parents gave him a home atmosphere where he could learn.

Mary followed her son to the cross. Imagine if you can – viewing the public execution of your child. Imagine a mob beating your child almost beyond recognition and then nailing him to a cross. It was a horrible deplorable way to die. Jesus' mother stood and watched it all. Her heart broke. On the cross Jesus was very aware of his mother's presence. He told his brother, "Behold your mother." I think Jesus was instructing John to take care of his mother. Children are aware of their parent's presence throughout life. They know when a parent is involved in what they are doing. And they know if mom or dad could care less about what is going on in their lives. We all do. I knew as a child when and if my parents cared and when they didn't. You did too. So many children are raised today by absent parents. They may live in the same house with mom and dad but mom and dad are really emotionally detached from their kids. The kids are doing their "thing" and mom and dad are in some other kind of zone doing their "thing." The tragedy of all of this is that families become lost when living in different emotional zones.

We all have our different interests and hobbies. Remember though, the family that prays together stays together. Jesus came to bind us together in love and truth. Honest communication in the home guided by prayer and loving God supremely can pull us together and pull us through the diversities of life.

The strips of cloth that Mary wrapped around Jesus would only be the beginning. She would spend the rest of her life in some way caring for her Son. God gave Jesus a special woman and a special man to care for him in his life. You may be a special person to a child or to somebody. God has given you somebody to love or to help in life. You are blessed if you have somebody who needs you. We all do. We all need the strips of cloth. We need the protection, help and guidance that come from the hands and the hearts of those that care enough to bind us in love.

CHAPTER SIX

Christmas is Wonderful!

His Name shall be called Wonderful.

On August 31, 1982 I watched as they pulled Jared Daniel, our first son, from Karen's womb by Caesarean birth. On October 23, 1985 I watched as the doctor brought Zachary Tyler out of Karen's womb headfirst. Both births were amazing sights to behold. The birth of our two children – two healthy baby boys. It was more than wonderful. I was so ecstatic about the births that I just picked up the phone in the waiting area and starting calling people. People that I was not even really all that close to. "We've had a son! He's doing great!" People that I called joined in the celebration. "You've had a child?" "Yes! Karen and I have had a child!" "Well, what's his name…and how much does he weigh?" It was fun as to how people overall responded.

People respond to celebration. When we are in a festive, celebrating mood people overall see the beauty of our pure happiness and rejoice with us. It's easy to rejoice with someone over the birth of a healthy child. It's a wonderful experience.

When Jesus was born shepherds and wise men would come to see Mary and Joseph and celebrate with them because the birth of Christ was wonderful. The Bible says his name shall be called wonderful," (Isaiah 9:6).

What is the most wonderful part of your life? Is it your job? Some people live for work and their jobs. I love mine. I love speaking to my church and other churches and groups. I enjoy writing and working with others to pursue their spiritual goals as well as educational and writing goals. I put a lot into what I do...but it's enjoyable for me. It fulfilling. Not all jobs are all that wonderful. But every job has something wonderful about it. Sometimes we have to look to see the wonder of it all.

Some people live for a relationship. My life for most of my married years has been about caring for my invalid wife. Half of our married lives Karen has contended with multiple sclerosis and being an invalid. Most of our relationship has been about seeking health, new medicine and overcoming mountains. There is something about mountain climbing that is breathtaking. While I don't prescribe adversity for any couple, trying times can make us see what the real wonders of life really are. There are some facets of life that we will only see from the mountainside of adversity.

The most wonderful part of your life may be your hobby. You love to fish, hunt, exercise or work with your hands. You find rest and relaxation. Your leisure time is what makes life wonderful for you.

The Bible says, "His name shall be called wonderful." What's wonderful about Jesus?

He makes every life wonderful. Regardless of your job, relationship or how you spend your leisure time Jesus adds a new flavor and a new perspective. He gives life. He gives hope and peace. He came and died on a cross so that we might be forgiven and cleansed of our sins. We were lost but Jesus came and found us. He left the splendor of heaven and came to earth to find us and make our lives wonderful.

Is your life wonderful? If not, try the following:

1. *Pray.* God will hear your prayer if you go to him in the name of Jesus. Jesus is the name that God adores and honors above every name. Go to God in prayer in the name of Christ. If you feel that you are lost and hopeless then ask God to fill up your life with His love, life and presence.

2. *Reconcile with God.* Sometimes we allow mistakes and sins to rob us of life. Life is no longer wonderful because we've made it so bad. We've goofed up. The foul-ups in life make us feel miserable. They deplete us of our energy to push ahead. So often many of these foul-ups are internal. We haven't necessarily wronged someone else but we have been wrong within ourselves. Try reconciling within yourself and with God. Simply say, "God I want to be right within myself. I want to do the right thing. I want to be at peace with

you. God will help you and add a sense of wonder to your life.

3. *Reconcile with man.* Life is not the best if we feel we have enemies or life is filled with ill will toward someone. Christ breaks down walls of animosity. Christ came to make us brothers and sisters. If there is someone that you are in conflict with pray and ask God to give you the wisdom to say the right thing. Pray for guidance to write the right letter or make the right phone call. We are to live in peace with people if at all possible. Sometimes it is not possible and we have to say goodbye to an acquaintance or friendship. These scenarios are difficult but on occasions they are the only way to live in peace. God does not expect us to live in a brutal relationship that cannot be reconciled.

4. *Decide what you want.* What do you want in life? Make it simple. Provide for your family? Finish your education? Make your job or business successful? Complete a project. Our lives so often fall into dismal swamps. We are unsure where we are going and we are unclear where life is going to be five years down the road for us. A goal gives our lives more direction. We have purpose to work toward something. Purpose brings about a daily wonder. God will help you - ask him to.

5. *Make every day a good day.* You only have today. You can't relive yesterday. You can't count on tomorrow. Enjoy today. Be constructive today. Don't waste your life starring at the television or the computer screen. Be active. There is a sense of wonder that God gives in Christ when we focus our energy on today.

6. *Take care of yourself.* This means spiritually, emotionally and physically. Exercise, read God's word and find someone with whom to have Christian fellowship. There are few people who will stand guard over you and make you care for yourself. It's your choice.

7. *Find the wonder in the smallest places.* Shepherds that Christmas night never dreamed they would encounter such wonder. An angelic host praising God, announcing the birth of Jesus, met these ordinary men. Jesus is that way. He has a knack for adding splendor to the most ordinary circumstances. Later they would find this wonderful Savior in a barn lying in a manger with peasant parents. This Christmas look for the wonder in the uncommon places.

Jesus made every life wonderful that gave Him the opportunity. Those who listened to Jesus learned. Those who followed Jesus witnessed miracles and changed lives. Those who touched Jesus were never the same. Those who sat with Jesus felt loved and forgiven. Those who saw him die on the cross exclaimed that surely he was the Son of God. Disciples who saw the nail prints in his hands and his resurrection cried out my Lord and my God! No one that has ever come into contact with Jesus Christ walked away doubting the wonder of this man. That's why at this Christmas season we can affirm the Bible anew and afresh, "His name is wonderful."

CHAPTER SEVEN

His Name

Shall Be Called Counselor

More people seek counsel today than ever before. We live in an unprecedented era of legal counsel. Marriage counselors work at an unprecedented rate. People struggle in the marriage relationship more than ever before.

We have tax counselors, financial planners, ministers who offer counseling, guidance counselors in the high school and college. Drug and alcohol counselors play a significant role in our society as the problems of abuse continue to plague society.

Everybody throughout life will need a counselor. Sometimes this counselor may be the person who helps you to discern. He or she listens and evaluates what you are doing and enables you to make discernment about further activity. Or someone hears about your problems and gives you counsel as to properly work toward resolving your problems.

The Bible calls Jesus counselor. Isaiah said he would be called "Counselor."

Jesus said when he went back to be with the Father he would send the Holy Spirit and he would be our counselor. The Holy Spirit is within every believer and he is our able counselor.

When Jesus came and he taught people. The greatest counseling we can do is to teach. When we teach we are giving people information and they act accordingly. Decisions are made based on their information.. Jesus taught his disciples and even the masses. Today we have schoolteachers, pastors and others who teach. How much counsel in your lifetime have you received from a minister that stood before you and others each week and faithfully gave you Godly instruction? It may be more numerous than you can recall.

While Jesus was here he was a demonstration. He demonstrated what God could do. He worked miracles that only God could perform. Bringing a dead man back to life is an act of God. Jesus proved He was God in the flesh. He was a demonstration of what God can do.

Sometimes our greatest counsel is not verbal communication as much as it is life demonstration. Jesus talked about God but he demonstrated God. We gain insights in how to do life by watching what others do and how they conduct themselves. People unknowingly counsel us by their good or bad behavior.

Throughout life we need counsel. A mom or dad might give us some direction. A good friend may offer some advice. Much of the time we have to look within ourselves. What are we going to do if there is nothing within us? I've had times in my life when I've looked within and couldn't find the answer. It's a very lonely feeling when there is no direction on the outside and no real sure direction on the inside. But it has been during these times that I have been driven to my knees in prayer seeking God's counsel. God has given to me the Holy Spirit as He has other believers. Sometimes God has counseled me by giving me clear direction. He becomes my counselor. On other occasions his counsel is only the peace that he provides that He is with me in the storm and that I should continue forward – He is with me.

Christmas is a time when we need the counsel of our loving Father. People have all kinds of troubles at the Christmas season. There is so much loneliness and depression during Christmas. Jesus is our counselor. Don't be down during the Christmas season. Allow Christ to lift you from your despair. Focus on Jesus. The angels made the announcement of Jesus' birth and the shepherds looked up. The wise men looked up guided by a star. Jesus was lifted up on the cross. In the tomb he got up and walked out. He ascended up into heaven. Christmas is about being up and never about being down and depressed. One of the way's the adversary of Christ gets into the birthday celebration of the Savior is by distorting it. He makes people feel bad because life may not be what we are led to believe that it should be. We think badly about life. We focus on our inadequacies. We begin to be depressed. Look up! Look up to Jesus and when you elevate your eyes he will elevate your disposition and your heart!

When Jesus counsels us he never leads us wrongly. God's word will never tell you to do anything that is wrong.

When Jesus counsels us he will show us the right way. Jesus said to his disciples in John 14:6 "I am the way." Sometimes we don't know the way. But he gives us the right direction.

When Jesus counsels, he comforts us. He gives us the truth. Jesus said, "The truth shall set you free." When we hear the truth and obey the truth it liberates us. Sometimes we don't like the truth. The truth can be sharper than a two edged sword. However, we can deal with the truth. We can work with the truth. Lies are dark and fuzzy. We are unable to grasp reality if we lie to ourselves about life. But Jesus counsels us by giving us the truth. The truth gives us life.

Isaiah the prophet, divinely led by God, wrote years before the birth of Jesus that someday he would be born and that his name shall be called "Counselor." Take your troubles to this counselor. Take your successes to this counselor. Take your life and lay it out before this counselor. He will give you a full spiritual examination like no other and what He tells you to do may surprise you. It might be something that you already know to do – he is just confirming it. He may totally take you in a new direction. This counselor is good about doing stuff like that. He changed the entire course of life for Saul, persecutor of Christians. He took Saul and made him the apostle Paul – greatest missionary of all Christendom. Know for a fact that if you go to this counselor you will hear the truth, get the right advice and your life will never be the same.

CHAPTER EIGHT

The Mighty God

The baby Jesus was laid in a manger that first Christmas. When the shepherds arrived they found Mary and Joseph and the baby lying in a manger.

The angel had just previously announced to the shepherds in the field who was born and where they would find him.

The baby Jesus was the fulfillment of Old Testament prophecy. The long awaited Messiah was born. This baby was God. Amazing? Amazing to us all that a tiny baby could be God. Look into the manger. What do you see? Do you see God? Is this how you have imagined God to look? How powerful is this baby? Is this baby able to create stars, living things and the sand of earth's shore?

Stand at the manger and ask Him to create something. Ask him to do a miracle. But wait, this little human being acts just like a baby. He is totally dependent on his mother to feed him and needs to be held. The stable shelter that was sought out by his peasant parents is his refuge from the elements of the night. His lodging will be wherever his father and mother provide. His clothing whereas it is strips of cloth or a decorative mid-eastern garment will be at the sole discretion and ability of his parents to provide. This little baby in many respects is like any other baby. Babies have all the needs that a new life requires – attention, provision, help, love and detailed care in regards to the necessities of life. How could this be God?

One of the many miracles of the Christmas story is that Jesus born, as a baby in Bethlehem was God. John chapter 1 teaches us that the word became flesh and dwelt among us and we beheld his glory! The baby in Bethlehem was God in the flesh. He left heaven in the form of His Son with the purpose of living on earth, among men with the purpose of dying for our sins. He fulfilled that purpose and arose from the grave to give us eternal life. Jesus came to earth as the mighty God.

Only a mighty God could arrange such a feat. Only a real mighty God could leave heaven, be conceived as a baby in a virgin mother's womb and enter the world as any other baby. The birth was so human! The birth was so divine! The birth of Jesus was only something that a mighty God could do.

In Bethlehem we see the God of this world lying helplessly in a manger. He was a fragile baby. He was vulnerable to pain and danger – so much so that Mary and Joseph would flee into Egypt for the safety of Jesus when Herod grew paranoid about a new king taking his place.

Where is the mighty God when he has to flee at the mere threat of a mortal king such as Herod? Where is this mighty God who has nothing but a cow's trough for his bed? How could anyone worship a God that is so mere human?

The baby Jesus demonstrated God's love for man. "For God so loved the world that he gave his Son," (John 3:16). Jesus was proof of God's love for man. God did not give mankind false hope or false promises. God gave man love. He proved his love. God gave man more than words he gave mankind Jesus. Jesus would spend his entire life demonstrating God. He would demonstrate God in love, in teaching, in miracles, on the cross and in the resurrection. He was the mighty God.

The baby Jesus related to mankind. He related to the common man. Shepherds came to see him. They were the most common of the labor force in this era. The wise men came from a long distance bringing expensive gifts to extend to Jesus. They had the financial means to travel and to give gifts. They wanted to adore the Christ child. Simeon was a prophet that had waited many years for the coming of Christ. When Simeon saw Jesus he knew that his life was now complete and that he could go on to be with God. Jesus met the needs of the common man, the affluent and the religious that awaited the messiah. Jesus spent his life relating to mankind. He related to a daddy that was a carpenter. He related to wealthy tax collectors and was invited into their homes. He related to the religious leaders of his day. Nicodemus sought him out at night questioning Jesus about the new birth. Jesus related to disgusting sinners that were on the verge of being stoned. He reached out in love and told them to go and sin no more. Jesus was a mighty God. He began to work at relating to man from the very birth process. He was born like any other man. Lived life like a man. And then, he died a real death, as no man should ever have to die. He died between two criminals and in the final moment one criminal received the promise of life with Jesus beyond the grave. Jesus on the cross was relating even the dark persons of this world. His message is that no one is completely too far-gone in this life for God to help. God has the ability even in the final moments of our lives to help and save us and give us hope and eternal life.

The baby Jesus gave a message of good news. Jesus came proclaiming good news to mankind. He came extending grace, love and hope. Before Jesus people were hopelessly lost in sin but Christ came giving a message of forgiveness. He taught in parables about forgiving others and giving people second chances even unto seven times seventy if necessary. Jesus reached out to adulterous women that others would not come near to in the daylight and looked at a sinner beating his breast saying, "God be merciful to me a sinner," and said that he was more justified than an arrogant Pharisee who bragged about his goodness. Jesus was merciful. Jesus extended love and grace to others. Only a mighty God could love and reach out to others that way that Jesus did throughout his life.

This Christmas season focus your eyes on the mighty God. He is an awesome God. He is the God of Bethlehem. He is the God of heaven. He is the God that loved us so much that he died on a cross and conquered the grave by his resurrection. But he is the mighty God that is very active in our daily life. He didn't just come and do his time and then disappear. He is so mighty that even at this very moment he is aware of what is on your mind and get this – he cares. He cares about you. He cares about your hurts, your needs and he cares about what you are going through. In his mighty way he is reaching out to you to embrace you and bring about calm in your life. He wants to bless you and give you direction for this day and hope for tomorrow.

CHAPTER NINE

The Everlasting Father

When I was a child the thought of Mom or Dad dying was not pleasant. It was almost unimaginable. My mother and father cared for us as children. They were both hard workers. At this writing my mother is now with our Lord and my Father is still alive. But the time will come when my father's life on this earth will cease and he too will go on to be with our Father in heaven. We all do...if we die as believers in Christ.

Our physical bodies die. The spirit lives on eternally. Our earthly father's die, but God never dies. He is the everlasting Father.

Isaiah foresaw the Christ child and said, "This child will be the everlasting Father." Isaiah was saying, "He will be God." Only God is everlasting. Isaiah described this child as being wonderful, a counselor, the mighty God, the everlasting father and the prince of peace.

Our relationship with God is everlasting. Strange thought. How many relationships are everlasting? I have not seen some of my high school buddies since high school graduation. I really loved some of the people with whom I attended high school. But we haven't seen in each other in many years. I may not see many of them in this life again. We even promised we would stay in touch. But we haven't.

I was very close to many of my first cousins growing up. But today I seldom see most of them. We've all become busy and we live in different places.

We all have made relationships in life that did not make it for a long period of time. They could have been relationships that were acquaintances or maybe they were very intimate relationships but things happened. The relationship soured. People went their separate ways. Differences could not be worked out and the relationship ended. It's a sad part of life. Marriages end. Children are given up to others and friends stop being friends.

Our wonderful God at Christmas time came in the baby Jesus. But when he came, he came to stay. God is the one relationship in your life that you can depend on. He will always be with you. He will never leave us. He is now and tomorrow.

God will not drop you because you have made mistakes. God will not turn his back on you because you have turned your back on him. God loves you even when you have been the worst you can possibly be. He doesn't condone sin. He doesn't want us to do bad things. He is working constantly to help us avoid hurt and pain. As humans we are good at plowing into trouble. We go headlong into pain and suffering.

We know better, yet we do it anyway. God doesn't give up on us.

We can break the heart of God and we do it so many times in life. But God has a heart to love us. He doesn't walk away when things get bad. We are prone to try to walk. People do it all the time. We walk away from adversity, heartache and disappointment. We want to separate ourselves from the things that hurt us. God hangs on. He is everlasting.

We can definitely break fellowship with God. Our attitude and sins can lessen our communication and power with God. However, God doesn't' give up on us.

Not only is God everlasting…but, He is an everlasting Father. The goodness of God is the result that he loves us as a father.

Jesus pictured God as the loving Father in Luke chapter 15. The story of the prodigal son is of a son that left his father to plunge himself into deplorable living. The son made a complete mess of his life. He was broken spiritually, financially and emotionally. Physically, his needs had become great. He finally decided to try going back home. Jesus pictured the father seeing his son coming in the distance and ran to greet him The father threw his arms around his son, kissed him, loved him and gave him the best of clothes to wear. The father threw a celebration party to welcome his son home. Jesus gave us this picture of God and taught us that this is how God loves. He loves as a wonderful father. Isaiah said, he is the everlasting father. This father loves us like this throughout eternity. He loved us this way in the beginning of time. He loved us this way when he died on the cross. He loves us this way today. He will love us as a father down throughout eternity.

This Christmas, remember that you have a Father. God is your father. You can always celebrate Christmas. There is never a reason to say, "I have no reason to celebrate Christmas." Or, life is so bad that I can't celebrate Christmas." You have a Father. He will not leave you. He is everlasting. Turn to him and embrace a Christmas gift that is everlasting.

CHAPTER TEN

The Prince of Peace

Peace. The very word conjures different imagery. To some it is a day away from hassle. Hassle can be found most any place. We can find hassle at work, the mall, the traffic, the airport and sometimes even at home. Hassle can be found even in places that we would least expect to find it – church.

Nobody particularly likes hassle. We may find it at the airport but we don't enjoy it. We get tired of it. We may find it at work but we don't enjoy it. We get tired of it. We may have it at home, but we don't enjoy it. We get tired of it.

Hassle is never particularly enjoyed regardless of its origin. We never say, "Oh this hassle is coming from my best friend. He is lecturing me constantly about my bad habits and how I need to stop. The best friend may be right but we seldom enjoy the constant admonitions. Or here is a supervisor who gives you a month to complete a project but then in two days starts asking "How much have you accomplished? Are you close to getting it done? Soon, we feel pressured or hassled to hurry up and get it over with.

Have you ever had someone to almost ride your rear bumper of your car? You start out on the highway. You allow yourself time so you don't have to push to where you are going. Suddenly in your rear view mirror a car is seems to be almost touching yours! You speed up a little but your distance between you and the other driver hasn't increased. The motorist is still almost on top of you. What started out as a pleasant unhurried drive becomes more hassled until the other driver passes you.

Life will always have its hassles. We will always have to pay the light bill. We will always have to stop and buy fuel or recharge. Standing in line seems to be a constant in life whether it is the grocery store, the mall or the post office. The car will always need serviced and there will be personal inconveniences that we have to contend with along life's way. There are times we have to go to the doctor or the dentist or fill out the income tax report. And, neither of them are life's greatest pleasantries.

Along life's way we need to discern between inconvenience, hassle and the real issues.

Most of life we contend with inconvenience. We have to stop at the post office and mail a package. We have to drive the car to the auto dealer and sit there for three hours while they service it. We are told we have made a mistake on our income tax and owe another five hundred dollars. The children have two ballgames to play in – at opposite ends of town. The family comes in from out of town to spend a night but they end up spending three. Life is filled with inconveniences.

Yet, it's the inconveniences that may make your life most interesting. If everything was convenient you would become totally lazy. If nothing required you to think harder, be more creative or even go out of your way sometimes what would be the consistence of your life?

We all sometimes envision a tropical paradise where there is nothing but sun and surf and cool drinks and beautiful scenery. Those are those special vacation moments in life. Yet, life was never meant to be endless vacation. If it was, we would never recognize it as vacation. Soon, even the vacation would become aimless and filled with drudgery. It's when we have to do our daily routines and work and deal with our constant inconveniences of life that we recognize vacation. It is then that we are able to go into neutral, recognize and appreciate the change of pace.

Sometimes in life we have hassle. Hassle is a step up from inconvenience. We understand the difference. We say, "This is hassle." Returning a sweater for an exchange the day after Christmas may feel like hassle when we've stood in line for an hour to find out we don't have our receipt or their exchange policy has changed and we need to do more to comply with the new regulations.

I felt a little hassled flying out of Newark, New Jersey when they went through everything in my suitcase and then even asked me to take off my shoes. A lady looked in and all over my shoes. I thought it was weird and then a month later a man was apprehended on a plane for having explosive material in his shoes that he was trying to detonate to crash that plane. Suddenly what seemed like hassle ended up just being an inconvenience.

Hassle is when we feel pressured beyond reason. We are inconvenienced to the point of exhaustion. We are placed under impossible scrutiny or forced to perform beyond a normal standard. The boss says, "If you can't give me twelve hours a day, five days a week, then we may have to fill your job with somebody else." Or you are told, "This is the deadline. If this task is not done by noon tomorrow you might as well forget the promotion."

Maybe your hassle is at home. Every day you are told how you do it wrong. Every day you are reprimanded for how you failed at cooking, cleaning or not having whatever it is done correctly. You may constantly hear that you don't make enough money. You need to find another job. You are not caring for us. You may hear constantly that you are too fat. Or, you aren't as attractive as the neighbor. And what seemed at first to be little digs, have become a grind to you and you are tired of the hassle. You recognize you need to improve but you need some help not hassle.

Life eventually moves from inconvenience and hassle to real issues.

A real issue is when dad is diagnosed with colon cancer. They have no choice but to remove a section of his colon. The doctors hope they can get all the cancer but only the surgery and time will be able to tell. Suddenly, whatever was an inconvenience or hassle becomes life threatening. We go to the doctor in hopes that he may be able to save dad's life. That is exactly what happened to my father when he was 60 years old. A section of his colon was removed but he was able to later have his colon reattached and he has lived at this writing 20 years past that experience that at the time was life threatening.

A plane ride may be a hassle. But when some lunatic has gotten on board and wishes to harm others then all inconvenience and hassle has turned into an issue of life and death.

It's the issues of life and death that enable us to see that the inconveniences and even the hassles of life are not impossible. They are only interruptions of life that challenge us and may make us pick up our pace to get everything done. When a real issue comes along, then having to stand in line for an hour at a restaurant is like a blessing – we have the ability and health to stand in line and the privilege of going out to eat. The airplane aggravation is stressing but yet we are able to travel and move about the country.

A Life issue is when we stand at the grave and bury a child. Within ourselves we scream out to God – "Why Lord?" A Life issue is when we may watch the sweetest and most talented person in the world debilitate from being a master pianist and incredible mother to no longer being able to even feed herself or touch her face. Within ourselves we scream out – "Why Lord?"

Jesus Christ was born in Bethlehem. He came to give us peace. He is the prince of peace. The inconveniences and hassles of life can be interrupters to our peace. The real issues of life can zap us to the point that even functioning can be almost impossible. Jesus came to help us. He helps us by giving us peace.

Jesus calms every storm that he addresses. When he was on the Sea of Galilee he said to the storm, "Peace, be still," and the storm obeyed him. He has the same calming ability in our lives. He doesn't always change or remove our life issues. So often they don't get better or may even get worse. His peace enables works within us. While the world may be falling down around us, he enables us to keep it together on the inside and that is not an easy task. It's easy to lose it on the inside with just the inconveniences of life. The hassles of life really push us. But the life issues can crush us.

Jesus came to give internal protection against being crushed. He is our internal crush protector. He fortifies us internally. His peace is our strength against our daily encounters that squeeze us beyond being able to function. With Christ we are able to rise above them. We are like the eagle in Isaiah in that God in Christ gives us some soaring ability. The soaring strength comes in His peace.

The Prince of Peace. He is your peace. During this season of the year allow his peace to calm, bless and fill up your life. You'll see your inconveniences and hassles a little differently. And you'll find the one who will enable you to know that there is a tomorrow beyond even the greatest issues in life that sometimes almost strangle us out of existence – death, divorce, unemployment, crippling illness, and other losses that sometimes take us to the brink of not being able to go on. He is our peace that enables us to somehow go on and find hope for tomorrow.

CHAPTER ELEVEN

Christmas Gifts

The greatest Christmas gift of all is Christ. Over 2000 years ago God gave his best gift to mankind – he gave his Son.

Jesus Christ was the gift that kept giving. In his earthly ministry we see God's gift giving to all of mankind – generously and graciously. On the cross he was giving ultimately. Hs blood drained from his body as Jesus gave all that he could give.

During this Christmas season it is good to be reminded that all of our gifts are not to be found under a tree or bought from a department store. They can be found in what has been done for us by Christ.

Christ has made it possible for us to be forgiven. This may or may not seem like a big deal to you but if you know you have erred in life sometime or another then this is a welcomed present. We all have erred – sinned the Bible calls it. "For all have sinned and come short of the glory of God," (Romans

3:23). We have made mistakes. We have done things that were less than perfect. We have said things...done things that we can't change or undo. But God in his love forgives us through Christ. God welcomes all who will repent of their sin and turn to him in honesty. Honesty means we confess to God what we have done. We confess who we are. We confess that we are sinners and have made mistakes. We ask for his help to live life more faithfully and dynamically. God wants the best for us. That's why he gave the greatest gift. The greatest gift is Jesus. Jesus was God's gift to mankind to prove that he wanted to be at peace with man. Jesus took all of our sins on the cross. Forgiveness is possible because of the greatest gift. When we open our lives to Christ we are opening ourselves to the greatest present of all. No one has ever given so much. He came offering himself – totally. When we receive him we receive all that Christ offers to us and on top of all of this we receive forgiveness of our sins and mistakes in life.

Christ came reaching out to us. He came extending forgiveness. This Christmas pick up the phone and extend your self. Call someone and offer yourself in love. Your call may be the beginning of enabling someone to experience forgiveness. All they need is a call from you that says, "I'm thinking about you. I just want you to know that you are special to me. I care about you. And, by the way, whatever the mistake was it's okay. I love you and I want us to be friends in Christ." That could be a very difficult thing for you to do. It could depend on the severity of the fault or the mistake.

Maybe a drunken driver killed your child in a car accident. How could you ever do such a thing? How could you ever offer forgiveness? Maybe your father divorced your mother and left you when you were ten years old. How could you ever do such a thing? How could you ever offer forgiveness? Maybe someone mistreated you as a young adult or child and you bear emotional scars from the treatment. How could you ever do such a thing? How could you offer forgiveness?

Only by understanding that you are a recipient of God's amazing grace will you be able to offer grace and forgiveness to others. Should you forgive someone of wrongs that they have done to you it will be by the grace and goodness of your heart. Just like God has forgiven you out of the grace and goodness of his heart.

There are many gifts God gives to us through the gift of Christ and forgiveness is one of the greatest. But don't be a recipient of such love and grace and not extend it to others. As God has given to you – give to others.

Christmas is about presents and gifts – good ones – real ones. Forgiveness, grace and second chances come to us from the heart of God. These are the real gifts of Christmas. Enjoy your gifts! Enjoy all that you have under the tree because of the one who died on the tree! Extend these gifts to others. This Christmas – give lots of presents!

CHAPTER TWELVE

Christmas Quality

The holiday season always brings with it some aggravation. There is more traffic, more people at the mall and more opportunities for people to spend more money than what they should so they might give more, have more and do more. Parties are planned whether anyone has time to go to them or not. On top of this we add house decorations to the to do list. There are trees and house decorations to put up and then to take down. It is as if we have a season ready made to contribute more stress to our lives. Few people today have to search for more stress. It seems to be a part of our society. We have our modern day technology to make our lives easier and better. Our lives should be more quality than ever before...but are they? We are in search for more to make our lives better.

Do we have our calendars so committed and our children so involved in so many events that we spend our lives meeting ourselves coming and going? We are like this – too busy.

We become so busy that we find ourselves doing and pursuing more yet all the while overlooking the important things that we already have. The smallest blessings we overlook and often take for granted. We are in search for more.

One Thursday afternoon on February 7, my oldest son called me at my church office and asked if there was any particular reason why our electricity was off. There had not been power outages that I knew about. There were no storms. "The electric company may have cut our power off," I replied. "Let me call." I did call and sure enough our power had not only been cut off but there would be no way they could turn it back on before the next day at the earliest. They would be able to turn it on if they had payment and a huge deposit brought to one of their payment centers by 7PM. I had just not gotten my utility bill paid. There had been meetings to attend, people to care for, worship services to plan, phone calls to make, letters and books to write, a house to keep, meals to provide for teenagers and much more. I had just overlooked my power bill.

I went immediately to the nearest payment center and paid the bill. I was assured that it would be back on by 7PM the next evening. That was 24 hours. It was February. It was cold. I got no sympathy from anybody at our power company. It could be turned on earlier in the day but they would make no promises.

The evening would be long. It would be dark by 5:30 ...and cold. My two teenage sons and I would kill some time at a fast food restaurant, I would work some in my office at church and they would practice their instruments. Buying flashlights before we went home we prepared for a long, dark night.

I was grateful that my wife who suffers from multiple sclerosis was visiting with her family in Dayton, Ohio. A house that would get down to 50 during the night would have been very hard on her. Transporting her to a hotel in her invalid state would have even been harder. I rejoiced for that blessing.

My sixteen-year-old son said while walking around the house with his flashlight, "You don't know how nice television and radio is until you don't have it." We would all feel a renewed appreciation for electricity when it came back on the next day.

We get so busy with life that we overlook what we really enjoy. The next night we would go to bed with the furnace working, the electricity had made it possible for us to have light, radio, television, a microwave, a washer/dryer, dishwasher, garage door opener, garbage disposal, alarm clock radio, computer and much more. We overlook all those items normally. We have moved on in life of search of more. What we have is nice but we search for more. In our search for more we overlook what we already have. What we have we do enjoy but we don't pay enough attention to it and we lose it.

Utilities are so very nice. But, monthly we have to pay the bill or we lose them. A car is very nice but we have to pay attention to it or it will become dysfunctional and shut down on us. A house shelters us from the inclement weather but years of neglect will run its toll and the house will begin to fall down around us.

In our constant search to do more and have more we should never neglect and overlook our present assets.

Christmas quality is not in what we might get. The quality of Christmas is in what we already have. Celebrate what you have. Celebrate the people who are in your life. Celebrate your present gifts. Trying to create more life, more things to do, more places to go, more purchases to financially obligate you to are not necessary. Take time this season to enjoy and cultivate the people who are already in your life. Enjoy the physical possessions you already have. Do you really need more junk? Do you need to spend money on stuff that you don't really need?

This Christmas look around you and spend some quiet moments enjoying all of your gifts. Look at the people in your life – a spouse, a child, other family, a friend, a place of worship, spiritual family, warm shelter, transportation, food and so much more. All that you may likely need to have a quality Christmas is already intact. Have a quality Christmas by celebrating whom and what you already have.

CHAPTER THIRTEEN

Christmas Trees

I remember fresh cut Christmas trees as a child. My grandparents normally had a cedar tree in the living room of their home. I remember the fragrance of fresh cut cedar filling the house. When I was just about twelve years old I spied a cedar growing on the side of one of our hills where I grew up as a kid. Throughout the fall I kept eying this fine looking tree knowing that Christmas time was coming. The second week of December with my parent's permission I chopped it down and dragged it home. Once it was covered with lights, icicles and bulbs it looked just like a Christmas tree.

When Karen and I first married we had a cheap little tree that we bought just so we would have one for Christmas. It was kind of cheap looking – because it was! No matter what we did with it or to it we had difficulty making it look good. It was sort of a sad looking Christmas tree. We used this tree for two seasons and finally dispensed of it for a real tree.

In 1983 Karen took off to the Florence Mall one day when we were living in Cold Spring, Kentucky and practically spent a week's paycheck of teaching school for a Christmas tree. When I came home on a Saturday afternoon it was up and decorated and she was beaming. The tree was gorgeous. I congratulated her on her tree expedition. She had done well. However, it was good that she went ahead and bought the tree I would never have consented to that kind of purchase at that time. We were struggling with a house payment and a car payment on a modest salary. A nice Christmas tree was not in our budget. That tree is going on twenty years of service. Every year we drag it out, shape it a little bit here and there…decorate it and enjoy it. The tree has stood the test of time. Karen's quality purchase has made for a decorative Christmas for the Mollette family for many years.

The Christmas tree is a fixture of the season. Even my elderly mother enjoyed putting up a small tree in her living room. There is something about a tree during Christmas covered with lights and decorations that adds to the celebration.

Jesus died on a tree. He died on a cross, made from trees. He was God's Son, who was born to die for the sins of mankind. I haven't seen many ugly Christmas trees but the cross for a day became ugly. The cross became the death place for the Son of God. The beautiful Son of God was cruelly and unmercifully executed in public before mankind to watch. The blood of Jesus covered that wooden cross. A soldier rammed a spear into the side of Jesus. People in the crowd hurled abusive comments toward Jesus.

As Jesus hung on that cross he was dying for your sins. He was the sacrificial Lamb of God. The sins of the world covered Jesus as he hung there with his blood draining from his body. There is nothing beautiful about sin. There is nothing pretty about my sins – how about yours? Are your lies, lust, thievery, foul words, gossip, anger, hate, and evil imaginations pretty? They don't sound pretty. No one's sin is pretty. Jesus was beautiful. But for a day sin stained the Son of God and he became ugly.

Three days later Jesus arose from the grave and later would ascend into heaven. As he appeared before the disciples their hearts would burn within them out of sheer delight at being in the presence of Christ. Jesus was that way. He attracted people. He was beautiful.

In Bethlehem it got quiet one night when peasant parents gave birth to a beautiful baby. Shepherds and Wise men would gather to adore him. We often sing, "Silent Night Holy Night." Angels announced his birth and stood watch. The Christ child was in the manger. Can you imagine the sheer beauty of a baby in a cow's trough? There would be another quiet time in the life of Jesus. When he hung on the cross the earth quaked and there was darkness that covered the earth for three hours. People got quiet. There is something about beauty that quiets us. There is something about the horribly ugly that causes us to get quiet. Jesus experienced both the beautiful and the ugly.

When we celebrate Christ we focus a lot of attention on a Christmas tree. Many trees in homes today are artificial. That's okay...they can still remind us that Jesus died on rough lumber from a tree. And while that tree on which he died shows man at his worst it loudly demonstrates to us God at his best. God gave us his best on the cross. The cross was expensive. The cross-contained God's best – His Son. And, for two thousand plus years that cross keeps touching our lives. The cross was not some cheap act of God. The cross was pricey. The cross was a quality act of God that just keeps standing against all time and keeps bringing joy and meaning into our lives. Where would we be today without the cross? What if God had not gone to so much trouble?

Those who fill up our lives with acts of kindness always make Christmas better. They teach us that we need to work harder at being better people. God filled up our lives when he by his grace came one Christmas. His kindness for us on the cross has forever changed us and made us better.

This Christmas, find new meaning in your decorated tree. Enjoy it and celebrate the fact that Jesus went through a lot of trouble to give you eternal life. What he did was quality and will stand the test of all eternity.

CHAPTER FOURTEEN

Any Room?

When Mary and Joseph arrived in Bethlehem there was no room in the Inn. For a couple expecting a baby this likely was discouraging. They had traveled and were tired. A place to sleep comfortably would have been welcomed. Inns in the first century were nothing like the very comfortable hotels we have come to expect today. The inn had few amenities to offer. No king size bed, whirlpool baths, or buffet breakfasts. This Inn may have had only one room with guests scattered throughout. If this was the case then it probably wasn't a good place for Mary to stay. There was no privacy and giving birth to her baby in such surroundings would have been very difficult.

The stable seems at first glance so harsh. Mary and Joseph had to sleep in a stable. There was no room for them in the Inn. At first it seems so unfair. Mary and Joseph would be bringing the Son of God into the world. The finest lodging in

Judea would only be appropriate. A cow's trough filled with straw in a barn would be unimaginable for the baby Jesus.

It seemed like every step of the way God was working in unimaginable ways. God coming to earth was unthinkable. Born of a woman to live a life that would end in the cruelest of ways was incomprehensible.

God's ways are not our ways. God existed before us and God knows the future a million years from now. We scarcely are passing through this world. We are briefly here and then we move onto eternity.

Yet, the barn was God's blessing to Mary and Joseph and His way of taking care of His Son. There would not be complete privacy in the stable but maybe more than the Inn. People would come and go but in a little makeshift spot the couple would seek rest and refuge in preparation for the expectant child.

Sometimes what may appear to be the worst of times may be the best of times. The adversities of life are never sought nor welcomed. We normally work to avoid hard times. But when they come and we can hang on and make it through them we look back discovering that we have learned. We look to God to help us through them and pray that we will never have to undergo them again. We compare the hard times with the good times and know there is a distinct difference between plenty and famine. We give thanks that God saw us through the famine and pray that we will never have to undergo it again. Hopefully, we will be more wiser and prepared next time so as to avoid such extremities.

We look at our misfortune and say; "I have to sleep in the stable tonight. But I'll never sleep here again." Or, "My baby slept in a cow's trough but he will never sleep here again." The adversities of life have a way of making us or breaking us. So often they work up a resolve within us that makes us more determined to overcome. There are those times when we are so broken we feel hopelessly lost. A case in point is the weary disciples that fled for their lives as Jesus, who was all they had lived for, was brutalized on the cross. For three days what they had believed to be real was over for them. It was not until Jesus arose from the grave and appeared before them that they were resurged with hope and new vitality.

Everybody has to see someway out. Everybody has to feel there is a sunrise. Somehow we all look for a little light at the end of the tunnel. All it takes is just a little light at the end of the tunnel to keep us going. If we can see just a ray of hope we are encouraged to keep life in forward.

God's messengers up to this point had instructed Mary and Joseph. Mary was told she was going to give birth to a child. The Holy Spirit would conceive the child. Joseph was likewise instructed by an angel, a messenger from God not to abandon Mary because this child was more special than any other child. Later Joseph would be instructed in a dream to take his family and flee into Egypt. I suspect that Mary and Joseph must have felt that God had brought them this far and that God would see them the rest of the way through. God did. God took care of his son all the way to the cross fulfilling his plan to redeem sinful mankind. When the job was done God brought his Son home. The disciples watched Jesus ascend into heaven.

The angels, again messengers of God, announced Jesus would come again in like manner

God has seen you to this point. He has the ability to see you all the way through. Adversity, hardships, mistakes and life's setbacks can be painful. But, we can learn from them and be better. We don't have to repeat our mistakes. We can learn from hardships and try to avoid them next time. Or, when the hardship is over we praise God that we survived the storm and now are able to enjoy the calm.

Even in the stable that night we sense God at work doing what he does best giving peace to unsettled hearts. When Jesus was born, the barn, the smell of animals and the uncertainty passed away. The focus of this peasant couple and all of creation was upon the new life that had come into existence. Jesus would forever change this couple as he would the world. While they would still face all the pressures of life they would now face them with their son. And the Son gave them an entirely different perspective.

Christianity never exempts us from life and its pressures. Jesus did not come to save us from adversity and hardship. Both are realities of life. But He came to be with us. When he came to be with Mary and Joseph life changed for them – for the better. When we welcome him into our lives we are welcoming Him and making room for him just as they did. And, our lives are for the better.

This Christmas season there will be many Inns, places and even homes where Christ will not be welcomed. Will you welcome Jesus? Will you welcome him into your home? Will you personally welcome Jesus? Welcome him again by saying,

"O Lord, I have welcomed you before into my life but just in case I haven't said it in awhile…you are most welcome in my life. Thank you for being here. You are so very welcomed into my house, my car, my office and most importantly my very heart and life."

CHAPTER FIFTEEN

Christmas Love

This Christmas love the people who are in your life. You may have a huge family…or one or two family members. You may have just one or two distant people in your life. Reach out to them and love them. Give them love. The world is aching for love.

Lonely families struggle for love. Husbands and wives both are burning the fast track going 90 miles per hour every day. Children have school and many activities that take their time. Sometimes love gets lost in the hustle of a fast life. This Christmas and every day of your life give love. Give love to those who are sitting right there in your very own house!

Receive Love. If someone is reaching out to you in love, let that person love you. There are boundaries. Sometimes people want to give you unhealthy love. It's like they are smothering you…trying to control your life. However, if people are able to offer you a Godly friendship that is filled with love then accept it.

God is love. Christmas is about God's love in his Son, Christ. When you look at the baby Jesus you see God's love. When you look at the cross on which Jesus died you see God's love. God's love was evident in all that Jesus did in his life and ministry to others. Jesus knew how to love. God knows how to love and He showed us that He knows how in Jesus.

How many people are in your life? A lot? A few? One? Nobody? If your answer is nobody then determine there is somebody you will love this Christmas. There is a neighbor that you might reach out to. There is someone at church you may extend kindness and love toward. Give love and you will be loved. Receive love and you will be fulfilled.

God came looking for us. He came to show us love. He came searching. He left heaven searching for you. He is the gentle and kind shepherd that sees you as vitally important to His kingdom.

This is what happens when we let God love us – we feel fulfilled. Are you fulfilled at this very moment? If the answer is no then please just take a moment and look to God and say, "God you are most welcome to love me! I will give you love in return."

Jesus told us to love the Lord your God with all your heart, soul, strength and mind and your neighbor as yourself. Jesus knew that what mankind needs in order to feel happy and fulfilled is to love God and love others. Love God at this moment…embrace Him and love Him now. Love someone else now. God will give you somebody to love if you don't already have someone. Ask Him to give you someone to love. If you have family then you have people to love. If you have a church family you have people to love. There are people all around who need your kindness and love.

Give love and you will receive love. Jesus said, "Give and it shall be given to you good measure, pressed down and running over shall people give to you."

Christmas is love. When Jesus was born, God was extending love to you. Receive His love and share it with others.

CHAPTER SIXTEEN

Giving Up
Before Christmas

Joseph almost missed Christmas. We can hardly blame him. The news of Mary's pregnancy was shocking because he knew the child was not his. Having a change of mind about marriage to this woman is not surprising. Who could blame him for changing his mind? Nobody. But God was at work and soon God through His messenger was revealing his plan to Joseph. Joseph would proceed with the marriage and share in the parental responsibilities of raising Jesus. He would be with Mary as her husband in the stable when the Christ child came into the world. God had to intervene because Joseph was in the process of changing his mind. He was working through the stress of giving up on his engagement. He was deliberating on going a different course.

We all do this to some extent. We throw in the towel. We resign. We take early retirement. We withdraw. We give up. We change our minds. Things change.

Mary's unexpected pregnancy presented Joseph with a changed scenario. It was such a drastic change of events he was going to cancel the engagement quietly and move on with his life – in another direction.

Only the power of God making his will perfectly known enabled Joseph to proceed.

So often this is what we know we need to hear – a message from God. We need His direction. Like Joseph if we know what God is doing then we are better able to proceed in life. We have a new surge of energy to go on with the plan or to make the right plan.

Galatians 6:9 "Let us not grow weary in doing well. We will reap a harvest if we don't quit." Life has a way of presenting challenges that make us quit.

What makes us give up?

1. *When it's more than we can stand.* We reach a level where the physical or emotional load is more than we can bear. We begin to second-guess our stamina or our fortitude for carrying on.

2. *The unexpected wears us down.* We deal better with the familiar. Plans change but drastic changes drain us. They stop us in our tracks and make us wonder, is it really worth it to go on.

3. *When it's not what we want.* We easily go forward when whatever we are doing is what we want to do. But when it's not what we want we advance slower. There is more drudgery in our actions. We get out of bed slower and it takes us longer to shower because there is no energy to face that which we really do not want to do.

4. *Failure to achieve some level of success.* We don't mind trying if we can experience some modicum of success. But when we plant and water and plant and water and there is no harvest, we grow discouraged and want to give up.

What makes us hold on and keep trying?

1. *The reinforcement of someone.* Someone who says to you, "You are doing a good job. You are really good at what you do." Affirmation of our efforts is a boost to our mental and physical energy levels. It helps if someone believes in us. It also helps if you will believe in someone. There is someone in your life that needs your emotional support. They need to hear you say to them, "You are really great. You really do a nice job. You are going to make it...stay with it."

2. *Role models who succeed.* Every person that goes forward can do it better if they have a courageous mentor. Everybody needs somebody they can look up to. We need the role models of life that may have gone through many of our similar trials but they found a way with God's help to survive and even thrive in their adversity. We see that they made it and we have hope that we can make it too.

3. *Prayer support.* Every one needs people who will love them and pray for them that they can make it. You can find this. You can't find it just anywhere. But, you can find prayer partners. They must be people who are unselfish. Not everyone is unselfish. Not everyone will pray that you have a great marriage; a great successful career or that you will even have a great life. Many of these people will not because they are so beat down themselves and may selfishly not wish you well. God has placed unselfish people strategically upon the earth. You can find a few in every community and most every church will have some unselfish people who will lift you up in real prayer that God might richly bless your life. Find a few real prayer partners that will wish you well in real prayer to God.

4. *Someone to talk to.* Not just anyone. The worst thing you can do is just talk to anybody. It must be someone who loves God and who genuinely cares about you. Don't trust your heart and life to just anyone. Be prayerfully discerning about whom you ask to share your heart's struggles.

5. *God's word and public worship.* God's word is a lamp unto our feet and a light unto our paths. His word gives us inspiration and direction. We are told not to forsake the assembling of ourselves together. There is a good reason for this…we need the fellowship of fellow believers and joint worship. A cinder from a fireplace glows for a while but soon burns out. Throw the cinder into the fireplace and it burns and glows with the rest

of the fire. We need the fire of public worship and the fellowship of other believers.

6.   *Rest.* I cannot underscore how important it is that you make your decisions when your mind and body are rested. You will think clearer. You will know better what it is that you really want to do. Jesus said, "Come unto me all of you who labor and are heavy laden and I will give you rest," (Matthew 11: 28).

Joseph almost missed Christmas. He almost quit before the marriage occurred and Jesus was born. With God's help he hung on and saw the wonder of the Christ child that was laid in Bethlehem's manger.

What is there about your life that has you on the verge of giving up? Will you hold on? Will you wait? Give yourself a chance to rest, read God's word, pray, talk to someone you trust and give real consideration to what is really best?

It could be that the very decision you need to make is to give something up and go another direction. There is nothing wrong with that. People change courses all the time. But just make sure you feel that what you are doing is of God and the very best decision for you.

Joseph would find that his decision was not of God and was not the best for him, Mary or even Jesus. Too many people were affected. But God was with him and helped Joseph to know what was right and he gave him the strength to do what was right.

He will help you to know too. Just make sure that whatever you decide that it doesn't cause you to miss Christmas.

CHAPTER SEVENTEEN

The Christmas Moment

There had to be a lot of anxiety within Mary and Joseph. There was a planned wedding. And then there was an unplanned pregnancy. Next the wedding is cancelled. And then the wedding is back on. Next they have to travel for a census. When they arrive, they don't have a place to sleep. They end up with a very humble place to sleep with no place to put a new baby but a manger. Do they remind you of your Christmas?

Too often Christmas is filled with anxiety. We become anxious about spending money. We may not have the money to spend. We may be on a very limited budget. You may be unemployed or your lifestyle has vastly changed this Christmas season. Or you may have plenty but the idea of fighting the traffic, buying for so many people, decorating, baking and all the demands of the season have you completely stressed out just thinking about it.

Before you know it Christmas has come and gone. You may rejoice when the season has finally ended and you can put the tree away. Before you know it ten, twenty and thirty Christmases have passed. The years fly by quickly. Our lives are like a mist. Life comes and goes and what do we have to remember? Too often we zone ourselves out mentally to avoid the pressure of the moment. We look past the present in anticipation of a quieter, happier future. While we do so we miss a lot of good moments.

How many weeks have you spent in dread and worry over an anticipated surgery? How many years of life have you wasted wondering, "How will all this turn out?" While we are waiting for the surgery and while we are wondering how all will work out we are wasting good and precious life. We waste the moment.

Before your life is over…savor a few moments. Savor a sunny day. Enjoy a walk. Smile into the face of somebody that you care for and share your love with him or her. Take note of your work and bask in the pride that you are capable of holding such a job and rejoice for every opportunity. Kick up your heels and clap your hands. Don't be afraid to be happy. Don't beat yourself up for a good feeling. Laugh and laugh out loud. Get by with every good positive, healthy and wholesome thing that you can accomplish because this moment will only last briefly and then it's gone. When it's gone we then have the memory of the moment. We have the memory of how wonderful it all was. Or, we have the memory of missing the moment.

Seize the moment and make it wonderful. Give it your best. Create a wonderful and happy memory. Fill it with smiles, good words and warm long embraces. Give life your best. You only get out of life what you put into it.

Mary and Joseph could relate to hassle. They would be able to communicate on our level about stress and pressure. They felt the tension of unplanned pregnancy and life uncertainty. We all get to go through these dynamics at one time or another in life. Regardless of our status we experience stress and some uncertainty in life. Sometimes we experience them at Christmas more than any other.

I've seen many Christmas programs during my life. Many Christmas pageants include angels, shepherds, wise men, animals, stable scene, innkeeper and of course Mary and Joseph. But at the center of the stage is always the baby. When the baby is laid in the manger and the congregation sings "Silent Night" it seems that everything becomes quiet and all is now okay. The hassled lives of these peasant parents now seem quiet and calm. On this very special night all the focus is centered in on this new baby – the Lord Jesus.

We should be careful to not let Christmas come and go with all the stresses and uncertainties without seeing Jesus. Don't miss the real important moment of the Christmas season – His birth.

Throughout the holiday do what is really important. Spend time with somebody you love and savor every moment. Write a card or letter to people who are meaningful to you and savor every word. When you are in the company of good people regardless of where you find them communicate good words and let them enrich your life.

In everything you do during this season of the year enjoy God's love and His marvelous gift to you – Jesus. His presence always changed life for everybody with whom he came into contact from Mary and Joseph, to a blind beggar, to a condemned sinner woman, to a Roman soldier who exclaimed him as the Son of God. He always brought new meaning to life and made every moment that people spent with him very special.

Take hold of Jesus today. Take hold of him right now...at this very moment. This very moment may be the moment of your life that changes all others for now, the rest of your life and even eternity.

CHAPTER EIGHTEEN

Follow the Star

Wise men traveled to see the birth of Jesus. "We have seen his star in the East and have come to worship him," they said. They followed the star until it led them to the Christ child. This strange phenomenon gave them the direction and the light they needed to find the Son of God. Yet, we should not be too surprised by the star. God made all the stars and the planets of space. How easy for God to provide a star to give direction to men who sought Jesus.

God wants us to find His Son. He did not keep Jesus hid in heaven. He sent him to live among men. Jesus lived, talked, taught and performed wondrous miracles that have been proclaimed down throughout the centuries. Jesus died in open public for the sins of man. More has been written about Jesus than any other human being. God has made Jesus very visible and public to the world.

The star gave light and direction. The star tells us about the nature of God. He will give you light and direction to

Jesus. He has given us the Bible. He has given us wonderful churches and ministers. He has given us untold numbers of inspirational/devotional books that tell us how to know Christ better and walk with him in a more devoted way.

These searching men found Jesus. They found him because they looked for him. They were men who were sensitive to spiritual things. They studied the stars. They knew the scriptures. They were watching for the coming of the Messiah. As they studied God's word and kept attuned to the stars they one day became aware that something marvelous had happened. The promised birth had occurred. Fulfillment of scripture had taken place. They saw the star. Their hearts were so thrilled they prepared to make a trip – a trip to worship and adore God's gift to mankind. They took gifts. These gifts may have been purchased at great cost. Or they may have been treasures they had set aside for a special occasion. When they saw the star they knew nothing could be more special than the Christ child born in Bethlehem.

A star led these men to the star. Jesus was the real star. God used a piece of his creation to lead searching men to the finest act of his creation – His son. Planet earth, the moon and all the stars we behold are marvelous creations of the mighty designing God. Jesus was his greatest work of all. In Jesus, we behold all of God – His love, grace and power. We would also behold all of man – joy, humanity and suffering. What a Star! What a Savior! What a God! What a man!

The wise men knew nothing less than joy when they saw Jesus. They felt drawn to the star because they believed it was leading them to Jesus – and it was. When they found him they were warned not to return to Herod. Herod wanted them to report back to him because he had wrong motives in finding Christ. He only wanted to eliminate Jesus. God directed the men not to return to Herod.

These men were led of God all the way. They found Jesus. They worshiped Jesus. They were then led away from danger after seeing Jesus. This is relevant today.

We will find Jesus if we want to. We will see Jesus if we seek him. God has given us his word, the church, special people who point us to Christ, so many wonderful books and inspirational "stars" who give us direction to Christ. All we have to do is open our eyes and hearts and we can see the way to Jesus.

There is truly direction for us in this life. Every day we need direction. We need to know the way for the day. Look to the star. Look to Jesus. Jesus will guide you. Look to him and you will find your way. "Looking unto Jesus the author and finisher of our faith," (Hebrews 12:2).

Set your eyes on Jesus this day and then you will see your way not only for today but suddenly the clouds will begin to part and you'll have hope for tomorrow.

When the wise men worshiped Jesus, God took care of them. God warned them not to return to Herod. The life of Christ could be in danger as well as their own. Herod was ruthless and could have easily taken the lives of these Godly men. After worship they had spiritual sensitivity that protected them from danger.

You will find it true for your own personal life. You will have better sensitivity to spiritual danger after you have spent time with God. He will be better able to lead you because you are attuned to him. Your eyes on the star make it easier for God to guide your life.

If the wise men had not paid attention to the star they might have missed finding and seeing Jesus.

Daily with our mind and heart on Christ we find new blessings, light for what we are to do and safety as he leads us away from danger.

CHAPTER NINETEEN

Learning
from Shepherds

Luke chapter 2: 8, And there were shepherds living out in the fields nearby, keeping watch over their flocks at night. An angel of the Lord appeared to them, and the glory of the Lord shone around them, and they were terrified. But the angel said to them, "Do not be afraid, I bring you good news of great joy that will be for all the people. Today in the town of David a Savior has been born to you. He is Christ the Lord. This will be a sign to you: you will find a baby wrapped in cloths and lying in a manger." Suddenly a great company of the heavenly host appeared with the angel, praising God and saying, "Glory to God in the highest, and on earth peace to men on whom his favor rests."

When the angels had left them and gone into heaven, the shepherds said to one another, "Let's go to Bethlehem and see this thing that has happened, which the Lord has told us about. So they hurried off and found Mary and Joseph, and the baby, who was lying in the manger. When they had seen him, they spread the word concerning what had been told them about this child, and all who heard it were amazed at what the shepherds said to them. But Mary treasured up all these things and pondered them in her heart. The shepherds returned, glorifying and praising God for all the things they had heard and seen, which were just as they had been told.

Showing Up Gives You Possibilities. The Shepherds were living out in the fields. So, they had definitely made a commitment of their time.

It's Important to Pay Attention. It sounds like they would had to have been dead to have missed this. But sometimes at our house the music is so loud there is no way I'm going to hear what is being said. I have two teenage boys and we have loud noise/music. If I really want to …I can zone in and hear what is being said. But 99% of the time I try to zone it out.

You ever do that with God? Zone out? Sometimes we can learn a lot …if we just pay attention.

Be Flexible. The Shepherds were flexible. The shepherds hurried off to see if what they had been told was true. Rigidity…concretes you…stations you to a lot in life that causes you to miss out on a lot of life's blessings. Sometimes you have to try something different. We get stuck in our routines. We feel safe in our routines. We don't venture out of our safety zones. But then we may miss the blessing. The shepherds could have said, "Aw that was something we ate." When we allow ourselves to stay stuck we miss out on blessings.

Some Days Are Different. The angels prove this to the shepherds. Many days are the same…but not every day. Aren't you glad? Life would be boring if every day was always the same.

We show up. We do the mundane. In the middle of the ordinary the unusual takes place. Show up at the word …each day. Mundane …maybe …but God may speak. Talking to somebody about church …mundane …boring …maybe …but sometimes God does incredible things.

In this story we read about…
Ordinary People. Ordinary Place. Ordinary Job. Ordinary night.

We read about an unordinary birth, unordinary announcement to these ordinary people. What made their lives extraordinary?

1. They showed up.
2. They were alert.
3. They were flexible.
4. They were willing to take a risk to see what this was all about.
5. Their lives were never the same.

CHAPTER TWENTY

Christmas Still Brings

(Matthew 2: 18 – 24)

Christmas always brings a certain amount of Unbelief. For most of us it is very difficult to believe that it is that time of the year. It's time to drag out that tree...or buy a tree if you use a live one. It's time to drag out those decorations. It's time to start getting those Christmas decorations out. And it is so hard to believe how time flies so fast.

September 11 was a day of unbelief. What we had never imagined could happen, did happen. We beheld what most of us would have said... "Impossible." The world trade center towers...both of them fell to the ground and we all watched it. Impossible ...but it happened.

None of us could have in our wildest imaginations weaved a scenario of such violence and terror to have believed that such deranged men could pull together such an unbelievable scheme to reek such devastation. But, they did. And our world will never be the same.

When would we ever have thought that the mail service could be dangerous? Evil people proved that mail delivery could be fatal as opening packages that contained homemade bombs killed several key persons. And now ...we have the Anthrax mailings ...and we have 94 year old women in places like CT dying from inhaling a poison into their system. Would you have believed all this ten years ago? I doubt that we would.

I think Christmas is always earmarked by a certain amount of doubt ...or possibly disbelief. Here we are again.

There was no way Joseph could believe what he was hearing. Mary ...we are getting married. We are engaged. We are committed to each other. I belong to you. You belong to me. We love each other. Mary ...we have kept our engagement pure. There is no way that you could be pregnant, Mary.

Who was he? Or ...who is he? What are you hiding from me Mary? Who is the other man in your life?

Joseph ...something strange is going on. I had this visit from this angel. And I was told that I was going to bring God's Son into the world.

"Mary ...what do you have in that eggnog? Have you been sick Mary? Are you on some medication that you haven't been telling me about?"

Joseph was obviously awestruck by this news and he had to feel a sense of disbelief by what he was hearing.

Christmas Brings Contemplation.

Christmas Brings Revelation.

Christmas Brings Anticipation.

Christmas Brings Celebration.

CHAPTER TWENTY-ONE

Characteristics of the Christmas Season

Matthew 2: 1 – 2

After Jesus was born in Bethlehem in Judea during the time of King Herod, Magi from the East came to Jerusalem and asked, "Where is the one who has been born king of the Jews? We saw his star in the East and have come to worship him."

Matthew chapter two reminds us of some of the characteristics of the Christmas season. We read about wise men, kings they are sometimes called but commonly referred to as astrologers …or men who studied the stars. They had traveled a great way, obviously gone to a lot of trouble, bought gifts and spent time worshiping the Son of God.

What can we learn from these men?

We can learn about the stress of Christmas.

Most of us do not need any courses or studies in Christmas stress. We don't need enlightenment any other time of the year. The wise men had traveled a long way. Possibly they had traveled for two years. Jesus was no longer in the stable as often portrayed in Christmas pageants. Jesus was in a house with his parents.

These men surely were tired. They had traveled several months or more than a year. These astrologers were tired. When they saw Jesus they had to be tired. This is where some of our church denominations were founded because most of the time when we come to church to worship Jesus we're already tired before we get there. Someone asked a man one time what kind of Baptist are you – Southern? American? Freewill? Hard Shell? The man said …I'm a tired Baptist.

We feel we aren't serving God and mankind and that we are worthless if we are not going and doing every minute of the day. We think there is some sort of sainthood reserved for people that never stop and that it's a sin if we rest and have some relaxation.

We spend a lot of our time just going and doing and spinning our wheels.

Whatever it is that you do …does it enhance your life? Are you a better person? Are you more useful to God and others?

So often times we work from a sense of guilt. We knock ourselves out thinking, "If we do more, go more and work harder then we feel redeemed or justified." We justify ourselves because of doing whether it is accomplishing anything or not. We feel redeemed because we are busy.

We are like the brother of the prodigal son …"I've worked so hard …been so good …been so perfect …I deserve a big party!" Yet, the sorry, no good prodigal son received a big party, new clothes and a big celebration. We are taught over and again that the just live by faith and we are saved by grace through faith.

A big part of the Christmas season is that we feel Christmas is not in celebration mode if we are not busting our skin at 90 mph. "It's Christmas" therefore we have to have a party. Or this is when we have to have our gathering. Of course they are all fun. Why can't we have a January celebration? We can sing "Hark the Herald Angels Sing" in January just as good as we can in December and we probably would feel more relaxed.

This is why I don't fuss at you when you go to sleep in church. You come here and it is the first time that you have sat down all week and got quiet and you are drained.

A man once asked his pastor, "Reverend, is there a little prayer I might pray before I enter in the sanctuary?" The minister, aware of the man's ways said, "I would suggest now I lay me down to sleep."

How will you stress out this Christmas? Too much to do? Too much travel? Too many places to be? Too much going and doing? Are you filled with unrest this Christmas? Fear of something? Worry?

Consider, secondly the guests of Christmas.

In Luke we read about Shepherds but it seems they gathered almost immediately. These wise men showed up later. It's always good for company to be spread out. If everyone comes at once you can get it over with but you don't have the opportunity to really savor each person's personality and what each one has to offer to you. I suspect that Mary and Joseph got more out of the Wise men's visit two years later than they would have if they had showed up with the Shepherds.

Is anybody coming to see you this Christmas? My dad will be alone this year ...but I have family who will dote over him during his grief of being without mother for the first Christmas.

It will be the four of us this Christmas ...but last year folks, I had to leave the Christmas Eve service and go home and load my wife into a car on late Christmas Eve and wheel her into a nursing home and put her to bed. And then on Christmas it was the same routine of going to the nursing home and checking out my wife and then returning her on late Christmas day. We praise God that we don't have to do that this year. Yet ...last year it was gravely vivid to me that so many of those people in the nursing home never left the place during Christmas. They did not have any cards or decorations in their room. I wonder if some of them heard from one family member. I suspect they sat there alone and if not for the tree in the foyer they wouldn't have known it were Christmas.

I don't think you should spend Christmas alone. Yet, millions do every year. Help out at one of the homeless shelters, or downtown mission. We have shut-ins and lonely people in our church. Attend a service; invite people into your home. If you want friends – be a friend.

I went out to find a friend and none could I find anywhere. I went out to be a friend and friends where everywhere.

These Wise men are remembered because they took the risk of finding Jesus. Had they not left home, we would not know them today.

Another characteristic are the pests of Christmas.

A big segment of this story involves King Herod. Historically remembered as being paranoid and violently mean. Herod told the wise men that when they found this new king to come back and report to him so he too could worship him. We know his motives were not pure. He proved it later when the wise men never showed up and he had all the male babies killed.

It would have been just as well if they had never met Herod. What good did it do them? What good was it for Bethlehem? What good was it for Mary and Joseph and Jesus? It was a bloody time for Bethlehem. Bethlehem was small and we don't know for sure how many boys were killed. Certainly it was not in the thousands ...but if it were only a few ...it was a few too many.

The magnitude of the twin tower devastation was overwhelming. Huge buildings and so many people were devastated. Yet if only one daddy had been killed in that building ...the devastation to his children and loved ones would have been just as great.

The wise men could have done well to steer away from Herod.

Do you know there are some people that you are better off to avoid? They judge you, they criticize you, they do not build you up but find ways to dig at you and put you down.

Why associate with them? Do you need that? You don't have to be mean to them …just stay away from them.

When Judas criticized Mary for pouring the alabaster ointment on Jesus' feet, it wasn't because Mary had a problem. She was just having a great time loving Jesus. Judas though, was a thief and self-esteeming, and critical. He had the problem and there was no way anybody was going to fix his problem.

Do you know that you can make yourself sick trying to make somebody else well? You just knock yourself out and they go right on and you end up beat and bruised.

The first Christmas had Herod. And every Christmas has a few pests. I think the biggest pest we battle is our secular culture. Every year we have to battle media advertising and traditional gift buying that makes many people feel they have not celebrated the season unless they have gone into debt to buy gifts. This year …try to avoid the Herods. They don't have your best interests at heart.

The Test of Christmas

Herod couldn't get through Christmas without killing somebody. How about you? Will you get through this Christmas without hurting someone?

Peace on Earth and good will toward men on whom his favor rests. Do you have this peace this year?

The Best of Christmas - What makes Christmas special?

The wise men were focused. They had one desire - to worship the newborn King. Could we this day refocus our lives and families on what Christmas is all about?

They did something with themselves. There is something to be said about finding something to do. We just said, "You can work too hard and be too busy." But sad indeed is the person who just quits. A new friend told me that at age 65 he couldn't stand it any longer and opened a small bookstore. Today at 73 he has outlived all his younger brothers and walks with a sense of purpose and enthusiasm about his life.

Make a pumpkin pie and give it to somebody. Go Christmas caroling. Enjoy the season.

The wise men gave. They gave the best they could. Giving comes from the heart. I haven't preached one sermon this entire year on tithing or giving. There are many in our congregation who give nothing. I don't understand if you have a job how you can give zero ...nothing. But our giving has been great this year because giving stems from the heart. When your heart is right you want to give something. You want to give of yourself, your time and your resources.

The wise men worshiped and admired Christ. This Christmas will be a Christmas of celebration if you will do the same.

CHAPTER TWENTY-TWO

Silent Night
When all is Quiet

How quiet was it when Jesus was born? The community was busy because people had traveled to register for the census. People were there that were not normally occupying the village. The Inn was packed. Yet, we sing the song, "Silent Night"? Could it have been a noisy night? Surely it was a frustrating night. No room in the Inn. Weary from travel. There was only a barn for shelter and straw for a bed? What kind of trip was this turning out to be? And now the birth pangs are incredible. There is no anesthesia. There is no doctor. There are no nurses. There is just a lonely barn and livestock and the stench of manure. This is not exactly a posh worship service with fine tuned instrumentalists and plush pew coverings with finely attired people whispering gently, "Silent Night, Holy Night." No, this is aggravation, pain and misery. This is public embarrassment. This was a stable. We have no idea how many of the Inn's people were in and out of that stable caring for their own livestock. You can just imagine the chatter in the Inn. "There is some poor woman out in that barn that is having a baby! What a poor couple they are."

When Jesus was born, life was not all that great for one peasant couple. They were away from home. They had very little money. Joseph must have felt bad that this little baby had to be brought into the world in such crude surroundings. He wanted to do the best he could in being a good husband to Mary and a good parent to this child. Was he failing? Was he feeling like a failure? Did he wonder, "Is this what God planned for me?"

We have all likely had these feelings. When life is supposed to be silent, reverent, blessed, holy and wonderful they are far less. They are noisy, filled with confusion, uncertainty and despair. We often wonder is this what God intended for me? Did God design this for my life?

We seek the refuge of Silent Night. We want the quiet, the solitude and the peace that we feel when we sing this song. We envision the newborn Jesus; blessed mother and marvelous father huddled almost saintly like in the stable. We imagine this divine moment and we know that God was at work in a small village, through ordinary people in an unusual way. We quietly feel the moment of that stable and we whisper, "O God, bring this feeling of internal joy within my life." We sing, "O come into my life, Lord Jesus. There is room in my heart for thee."

While there must have been an element of noise and confusion about the Bethlehem community there were supernatural occurrences that transformed the entire evening. God was at work. He was sending His messengers to shepherds in the field who were watching their flock. Angels were very attuned to Mary and Joseph and the new baby. The divine Son of God, not just any child, lay in the manger. All of creation grew quiet as this child, who came from heaven entered sinful earth, not in the palace of a king, but the temporary shelter of peasant parents.

When Jesus was born and lay quietly in that manger, Mary and Joseph surely felt a sigh of relief. They were finally in Bethlehem. The trip was over and Mary made it without harm to her or the child. The baby was now finally born. The mother is finally able to breathe a sigh of relief. Joseph beholds the child in astonishment as any parent beholds his new son. Truly this child is special Truly this child is of God. Suddenly within a few minutes the night is filled with awe and reverence and it overwhelmingly becomes a silent night.

Your Christmas may be filled with confusion and busyness and nonstop activity. Your days may be almost overwhelmed with exhaustion as you proceed through your daily life or work, events, family, sickness, church, bills and the list may be endless. When Christmas finally comes allow the divine Son of God to bring some quiet into your life. He transformed a peasant couple's life into a holy night. Allow Christ at this very moment to transform you and bring quiet into your life.